The Dream of Jesus

FATHER GERRY CLEERE

CAMPUS PUBLISHING

ISBN 1 873223 80 3

First published December 1992

Typeset by Irish Typesetters, Galway
Printed and bound in Ireland by Colour Books Ltd.

Cover photograph courtesy of Anthony McGeehan,
Bangor, Co. Down

Published by
Campus Publishing Limited
26 Tirellan Heights
Galway
Ireland

Contents

The Dream of Jesus

"To live is to change, and to be perfect is to have changed often." So said Cardinal John Henry Newman (1801–1890), and in July of 1991 I consoled myself with these sentiments as I struggled to come to terms with my third change after just six years of priestly ministry.

At the time I was a curate in St. John's Parish in my native city of Kilkenny and I considered it to be as near perfection as I would ever get. I was living and working with a great team of priests, parish sisters and lay people. Every day was full and each day was different. There was always some project in hand as well as some new plan being hatched. We had a dream for our parish and its people. It was the dream of Jesus, and we were trying to make it come true.

Then the telephone rang. It was the bishop and he wanted to see me. I remember having a fair idea what it might be about as it was that time of the year when every priest becomes suddenly alert to the possibility of change. However, I never imagined that I would be invited to accept the challenge of a temporary loan to the diocese of Down and Connor in Northern Ireland. We had a long discussion, during which the bishop filled me in on the background to the invitation and we talked about the reasons for and against accepting. In the end we both agreed that the reasons "for" far outweighed those "against".

In the days that followed I waxed philosophic about the need for all of us to be open to change and to God's plan for our lives. I talked about the value of choosing "the road less travelled". I told people that the priest had a particular duty in this regard, and I insisted that it was all part of the dream coming true. However, no amount of philosophising or dreaming could lessen the pain of parting when it came to leaving familiar and much-loved faces and places behind so as to "launch out into the deep".

What did serve as the perfect antidote was my subsequent appointment to the parish of Holywood in Co. Down. There I was blessed with a parish priest, Fr. John Stewart, who was wonderfully kind and caring, a fellow-curate, Fr. Anthony O'Connor, who was in all ways warm and welcoming, and a people who were enthusiastic and full of faith. My appointment to Holywood was also temporary, however, and it came to an end after just twelve memorable months.

At the time of writing this I am fresh into my new assignment at St. John's Parish, Falls Road, Belfast, and I'm already learning to love both the place and its people.

Since coming to live and work in the north of Ireland I have been asked a number of times to write or to talk about the experience and about the "northern situation". People have been anxious to hear or to read something conclusive being said about the north by someone from the south. On each occasion I have politely declined and I am still averse to doing so, on the basis that 14 months is by no means a sufficient length of time within which to draw any firm conclusions about so complex an issue as "the troubles". If there *is* anything I have learned over the past year or so, it is the importance of exercising some custody of the mouth and mind when it comes to expressing views about the north of Ireland in any public forum.

This is not to say that we can shed all sense of responsibility or feeling of concern for what is happening in Northern Ireland. This is particularly true for all who live in the 26 counties. There is in the north an authentic struggle for justice and peace and it deserves all the moral and spiritual support the people of Ireland can muster.

It is not to say either that I have not been deeply impressed by things I have seen since coming here. Nor is it to suggest that I haven't formed any convictions or conclusions about the people of Northern Ireland, because I have. In particular, I have been deeply impressed and humbled by the many miracles I have seen. I don't mean miracles of the very dramatic kind, although they may well happen too. The miracles I have been privileged to witness are of the everyday sort. Yet they are not always visible to the naked eye. Sometimes it takes the eye of the soul to discern their presence. What are these miracles that I speak of?

There is the miracle of laughter, the innate sense of fun which northerners have in abundance: their ability to smile despite so much adversity and danger, an ability which I am told is their antidote to insanity. There is the miracle of people overcoming death and tragedy and learning to embrace life again, and there is the miracle of those who help them to do this. There is the miracle, too, of a people who struggle with the frailty of the human condition and who try to be authentic Christians. There is the miracle also of people who live in the shadow and shelter of each other, who are good and kind neighbours, especially in times of need.

Most of all, there is the miracle of their stubborn spirit, a spirit which refuses to be broken, despite every attempt to do so, a spirit wherein hope springs eternal, a spirit which flies in the face of all that is evil. It is precisely this stubbornness which makes Northern Ireland most miraculous.

It is this same stubborn nature which helps its people to persist in the belief that peace will come. It is, in short, the dream of Jesus, a dream that is already coming true.

Helen's Story

I have a friend called Helen. (That's not her real name, but we'll call her that!)

We made contact for the first time about six years ago through a weekly programme I was presenting on local radio. One week we were discussing people's phobias and Helen wrote to tell us about a particular phobia which she had endured for quite some time.

She suffered from a condition known as "agoraphobia", an abnormal dread of open spaces, the effect of which was to keep her confined to her own home all the time.

A subsequent visit to Helen revealed that she lived with her parents and grandparents. Her father was unemployed, her mother was an alcoholic in recovery, and her grandparents were simple honest-to-God kind of people.

Despite so much hardship it was a very happy home, warm and welcoming, and we spent a lovely first evening together. I noticed from the start that Helen had a great relationship with her parents and grandparents. She told me that she was 17 years of age then; her condition first manifested itself soon after beginning secondary school. At the age of 15 she was forced to leave school for good, not by anyone in authority but simply because of the fear that had now taken control of her life. Her premature departure from school came as a great disappointment to all, for Helen had by that time proved herself to be a person of great academic promise and was highly thought of by all her teachers.

The previous two years Helen had been living in enforced enclosure, a life of quiet desperation that only her family knew all about. During all of that time she never lost her faith in God; if anything, it deepened all the more. She insisted that He would help her and heal her in His own time.

I told her that I admired her faith but suggested that God was already helping and healing a lot of people in similar situations through others who had been specially trained for the task. Helen knew what I was getting at, but seemed afraid of taking the risk, of launching out into the deep. I knew that we weren't going to reach any decisions after just one meeting and so we agreed to meet again, and again, until, in time, Helen agreed to seek some professional help, while at the same time maintaining her strong belief in the power of prayer.

Today, six years later, Helen is a changed person. She works in an office and devotes a lot of her free time to a self-help group for people with similar problems.

She still has a good prayer life, and has since helped to set up a prayer group for young people. Most important of all, Helen enjoys a degree of self-acceptance which she never knew before. Coupled with this self-acceptance is a firm trust that God has a plan for her life.

In a letter which I received only last week she writes:

> I'm resigned to leave it all in the Lord's hands. I'm blessed to be as well as I am, and after being through all I have been through, I'm more blessed than most, so I'm not going to be too ambitious. Anything will do, as long as I keep well. I don't mind after that. I know once I used dream of being someone important when I grew up. I wanted to be a singer or on T.V., someone that everyone would admire and look up to. The Lord however has made it quite clear to me, and says this to me many times in my heart: "Helen, if you want to be the first and greatest in my kingdom, then you must become the smallest and least important person in the eyes of this world". I see girls I went to school with in big jobs, going to colleges, travelling and enjoying their lives to the full. I don't envy them like I used to, for I know that in this world I'll always have to settle for second best when it comes to being successful in the eyes of the world.
>
> My biggest ambition now in life is to someday be happy and secure in my mind. To have a job, and husband and family of my own. I pray to God earnestly to send me a Christian partner, someone who will have God in his heart, and be loyal and faithful to me. I prayed for friends when it

seemed that I'd never have anyone and God answered me by sending me true friends who, because they loved Him, loved me with His love.

I ask you to pray for these intentions for me. I'm not anxious because I know God has a plan for my life and only God's will can prevail.

Helen's letter gives me hope, the sure hope that no problem is insurmountable and that all things are possible with God. If you are struggling with something difficult at this time in your life, just rest assured that God has a plan for you too, and that He can help you to overcome or to live with whatever it is.

Helen's story, and her letter in particular, have helped me to put things into perspective in my life, to get my priorities right, to realize that I am inclined to be ambitious for all the wrong things, and that what I want is not always the same as what I need.

Giving Without Measure

A few years ago I spent a summer working in London with some friends. It was a particularly fine summer: we spent our lunch-breaks taking the sun in the local public park. Quite often our peace would be disturbed by some member of a religious group, invariably the Jehovah Witnesses, going from bench to bench, seeking to convert a few souls.

One particular day I remember quite vividly. A young woman was doing the rounds, looking for a hearing. Almost everywhere she went she received a hostile reception and was told to "clear off". One old lady sitting on the bench next to us was particularly abusive, using language that shocked even *our* broad minds!

Eventually, the young woman arrived at our place and proceeded to introduce herself as a member of the Jehovah Witnesses. She continued with a well-rehearsed but nonetheless sincere speech. One member of our group decided to "give her a run for her money" and there followed a lengthy and at times heated discussion which must have lasted for all of thirty minutes, halted only by the signal for a return to work.

I could not but admire the sheer persistence and dedication of the woman to her cause, in the face of such adversity and downright abuse. I thought to myself: I wonder would I have the necessary courage of my convictions or thickness of skin to do what she did so well. And, in fact, I still cannot but admire Jehovah Witnesses and others for their dedication to a cause, whatever their religious beliefs.

I am often struck by the manner in which we all dedicate ourselves wholeheartedly to some relatively trivial pursuit like sport, socialising, etc., as well as to some of the more serious things like making money, doing a job, acquiring possessions and so on. And the thought occurs to me: if only we would give as much attention to the things which concern the soul, we would be much better people. If only we were as eager and ingenious in our attempts to attain goodness as we are in our attempts to attain money and comfort, we would be much happier people.

Our Christianity will begin to be real and effective only when we spend as much time and effort on it as we do on our worldly activities. Serving God can never be a part-time or a spare-time job. Once we choose to serve God, every moment of our time and every atom of our energy belongs to God. God is the most exclusive of masters. We either belong to him totally or not at all.

This does *not* mean that we should down tools and flock to monasteries or convents. It simply means that we give ourselves completely to God in the bits and pieces of life.

How Human Life Is Cheapened

We hear a lot of talk these days about how human life is so often "cheapened". The obvious examples spring to mind—abortion, euthanasia, prostitution, slave labour, "video nasties", child abuse, rape, murder and violence.

But there are many more less obvious and sometimes more subtle examples. And they're a lot closer to home. For example, that particular brand of murder and madness whereby supposedly sane people go around killing men, women, and children in the name of freedom. They assure us that it's all part of "the struggle", and occasionally they apologise when they murder the wrong people. Meanwhile, there are those who are their secret admirers. They quietly jump for joy at the atrocities they perpetrate, and offer unqualified support to this cheapening of human life.

Then there's the so-called "gutter press", those cheap and taste-less tabloids which have made a profession out of destroying people and cheapening human life. And we for our part lap it up. We buy these papers in our thousands. Therein lies the real pity of it all, that we don't have the good sense to discern truth from falsehood, fact from fiction.

There's our habit too of setting ourselves up as judge and jury, casting aside the age-old principle of "innocent until proven guilty". We jump to conclusions about people, passing sentence on them without the slightest regard for their good name or ever considering that they may not be guilty after all.

Coupled with this particular way in which we cheapen human life is our stubborn refusal to let people off the hook. We cling to the memory of things they have said or done and afterwards regretted, mistakes they have made and paid dearly for. We keep it "in for them", never letting them forget, and add in this way to our memory bank of malicious gossip.

Finally, there are the people who knowingly sell alcohol to underage and foolhardy youths so that the young can bury their boredom for a while and they can bury their ill-gotten gains. This too is the cheapening of human life.

These are just a few "close-to-home" examples that come to mind. My intention in mentioning them is not to "give out for the sake of giving out". Nor is it my intention to depress people with a catalogue of woe.

My purpose is to remind all of us—myself included—that we share a responsibility to root out those things which do not make for peace, the peace which Jesus of Nazareth came to bestow. He came not to cheapen life but to enrich and enhance life all the more.

In our great need we must turn to Him and ask for direction. He is always close at hand, wanting and waiting to help us and heal us. Let us not overlook his peace-giving presence, his guiding influence.

The story is told of a man who was lost in the desert. Later, when describing his ordeal to his friends, he told how, in sheer despair, he had knelt down and cried out to God to help him.

"And did God answer your prayer?" he was asked.

"Oh, no! Before He could, an explorer appeared and showed me the way."

We need to lift the blindness that often prevents us from recognising the closeness of Jesus, and how he is the answer to our prayers, and how he will show us the way—a better way.

Letting Go of Life

I remember a song which went: "Everybody wants to go to heaven but nobody wants to die."

And it's true—we all savour the thoughts of a life in heaven but we dread having to die to get there.

Which reminds me of an old joke where one man asks another: "Why do they build fences around graveyards?"

The answer comes: "Because people are dying to get in".

And people are dying to get into heaven. It's a case of having to.

Most of us have difficulties with death. It's certainly not a subject we easily warm to or understand. This obviously has something to do with the amount of pain and suffering often endured by the person who dies, as well as the grief and anxiety endured by those who are left behind. In this way death is destructive. Death is also a mystery. It is something which we can never hope to understand fully until we experience it for ourselves.

The only thing we can say about death with certainty is that it will come for all of us. Written around the dial of a clock in a church in France are the words: "One of these hours the Lord is coming." It is a sobering thought. We are given the same gentle reminder by Christ himself, who warns us: "Stay awake, because the Son of Man is coming at an hour we do not expect."

On some unknown day and at some unknown hour we will die. We know this, but it is hard for us to face the fact that our bodies, so full of life now, will rot and decay. We dread such thoughts.

Death is not just an event to be dreaded, but also an event to be prepared for, even to look forward to. There will always be these two tensions about death, its positive and negative aspects. W.B. Yeats, in his poem "Easter 1916", wrote: "A terrible beauty is born". Yeats considered the rising of 1916 to be something terrible because of the many young lives lost, but something beautiful because of what it would lead to—freedom for Ireland and its people.

There is a sense in which every death is a "terrible beauty". What's terrible about death is the pain and suffering involved for the one who dies as well as for those who are grieved. What's beautiful about it is what it leads to—life everlasting.

Yet still we cling to this life. We want to get to heaven, sure, but we don't want to die.

Consider this little story which I came across in *The Far East:*

> A child once asked his grandmother why death should involve so much suffering. In reply she asked him to sit on a chair and hold on tightly. "I'm going to try and pull you out." she said. A strong woman, she pulled until he thought his arms would fall off, but he held on for all his worth. Finally she wrenched him out of the chair. "That hurt, Gran," he said. "Let's try it again." she said, "but this time don't hold on." He did as she asked, and this time there was no struggle, no pain. His grandmother lifted him easily and gently out of the chair.

Day by day we must let go of ourselves by living for others. Then death cannot terrorise us. We may never be able to overcome our natural fear of death and decay but in our heart's core will be the peace and assurance that death is not so much the last experience, but the "At last!" event. At last I am to meet face to face the One Who has loved me and Whom I have loved here on earth. What more could we want?

What's Life Without Friends?

Alice Taylor, author of *To School Through The Fields*, once told me never to suppress a good impulse, and I thought it was sound advice. Ever since then I have tried to put it into practice.

Like that time when I was in London and I remembered that I had an old friend living in Ealing whom I hadn't met for at least 10 years. On impulse I picked up the telephone and we arranged to meet. We were old school friends, very close when we were both in our teens. Then she went to London, I went on for the priesthood, and we lost contact. We had both changed a lot in the meantime. But the extraordinary thing was that our friendship hadn't seemed to change at all. We took up almost exactly where we had left off 10 years before. We talked freely about our ups-and-downs, likes and dislikes, successes and failures. Then the time came for us to part once more and to go our separate ways. As we did, I think we both felt better that somewhere in the world we each had a good friend.

In a world that is becoming daily more impersonal, where the great enemies are loneliness and anonymity, we need friends and friendships more than we seem to realise. In true friendship people can find unconditional love and mutual acceptance; they can afford simply to be themselves for a change.

People nowadays complain about the loss of identity. Perhaps what they are really suffering from is loss of friends. Only with our friends can we really be ourselves. Who else but a friend would love us enough to tell us the truth about ourselves? Who else would get away with it?

There are many reflections on friends and friendship. Some are of the "mushy marshmallow" variety while others are much more credible, such as this one:

> A friend is a person who is for you always . . . He wants nothing from you except that you be yourself. He is the one being with whom you can feel safe. With him you can utter

your heart, its badness and its goodness. Like the shade of a great tree in the noonday heat is a friend.

Like the home port with your country's flag flying after a long journey is a friend. A friend is an impregnable citadel of refuge in the strife of existence. It is he that keeps alive your faith in human nature, that makes you believe that it is a good universe. He is the antidote to despair, the elixir of hope, the tonic for depression . . . Give to him without reluctance . . .

(Anonymous)

Friends and friendships were important in the life of Christ. The Gospels mention a family in Bethany, where Jesus liked to visit. It was the home of Mary and Martha and their brother, Lazarus. These were friends of Jesus and he loved their company. His disciples were also his friends. All these people were very important to him. If Christ needed friendship in his life, then who are we to assume that we can survive without friends?

Light One Candle

Over forty years ago an American priest, Fr. James Keller, founded a movement called "The Christophers". It was founded on the ancient but powerful idea that "it is better to light one candle than to curse the darkness".

What the founder of The Christophers was talking about was the power and influence of the individual, a power and an influence which we often tend to underestimate.

"In human affairs", said James Keller, "practically everything which has ever been accomplished for good or evil, throughout the world, began with one individual person."

It is documented history that the infamous Cromwell became master of England by one vote. It is documented history too that English became the official language of the United States by one vote. It is also historical fact that Charles I of England was sent to death on the gallows by just one vote, and that Adolf Hitler became leader of the Nazi Party by just one vote.

The great and vital defence of our natural environment, which we must all be a part of today, began with one lady, Rachel Carson, writing a famous book called *The Silent Spring*. The world-wide civil rights revolution began with another lady, Rosa Parks, refusing one morning, as a black, to move to the back of a bus. The Nobel Peace Prize began with one man, Alfred Nobel, the inventor of dynamite, deciding one day that he did not want to be remembered as a "merchant of death" and that he would channel his money and efforts to make peace in the world.

Such historical facts and examples all affirm that the whole course of history has been changed, more than once, by just one person. They also affirm that all growth, whether for better or for worse, is from small beginnings.

In the history of the world, surely the most outstanding example of great growth from humble beginnings is the life of Jesus of Nazareth.

One Solitary Life

Here is a young man who was born in an obscure village, the child of a peasant woman. . . . He worked in a carpenter shop until he was thirty. . . . He never wrote a book. He never held an office. He never owned a home. He never had a family. He never went to college. . . . He never did one of the things that usually accompany greatness. He had no credentials but himself.

While he was still a young man the tide of public opinion turned against him. His friends ran away. He was turned over to his enemies. . . . He was nailed to a cross between two thieves. While he was dying his executioners gambled for the only piece of property he had on earth, and that was his coat. When he was dead, he was laid in a borrowed grave through the pity of a friend.

Nineteen centuries have come and gone, and today he is . . . the leader of the column of progress. I am far within the mark when I say that all the armies that ever marched, and all the kings who ever reigned, put together, have not affected the life of man upon this earth as has that One Solitary Life.

(Anonymous)

"It Was None of My Business"

The year was 1941, the place, a Polish village called Minsk.

Adolph Eichmann, Hitler's specialist for Jewish affairs, had been sent to witness the extermination of 5,000 Jews. The morning was cold, The condemned men, women, and children undressed down to their underwear or their shirts. They walked the last 100 yards and jumped into a pit that had been prepared for them. Eichmann was impressed by the fact that they offered no resistance, apparently by this time reconciled to death.

Then the rifles and machine pistols opened fire. Children in the pit were crying, clinging to their parents. Eichmann saw one woman hold her baby high above her head, pleading: "Shoot me, but please let my baby live! Take my baby! Please take my baby!"

Eichmann had children of his own. For a moment he felt a twinge of compassion.

He almost opened his mouth to order: "Don't shoot. Hand over the child."

Then the baby was hit.

Years later, when Eichmann was eventually tracked down and arrested, he was found to be perfectly sane. He summarised how he felt about the mass-execution programme that destroyed some six million Jews with the following words: "I was a little cog in the machinery of the Reich. I merely carried out orders. After all, the people who were loaded on trains and buses for extermination meant nothing to me. It was really none of my business".

It is truly frightening to think that perfectly sane people are capable of doing such immense evil. After all, we look to the sane to save the world from madness and destruction. And now it begins to dawn on us that maybe we have more to fear from the sane than from the insane.

Which brings us to the people who put Christ to death—some of whom, namely the scribes and pharisees, Jesus condemns in the

Gospel for their hypocrisy. We have always tended to see these as a uniquely evil bunch who were acting from the vilest possible motives. This is a mistake, because all the evidence suggests that they too were perfectly sane people.

Perhaps it begins to dawn on us that we too have a lot to fear from ourselves and the evil we are all capable of doing. As Jesus warned: "It is from within that evil intentions emerge." Let us not fail, then, to recognise the fact that dark evil sleeps in us all, that all of us are capable of playing the roles of those who put Christ to death on Calvary, of those who put him to death again in the extermination camps of World War II.

Let us turn to that same Christ and ask him to save us from ourselves, and to help us confront and overcome the evil within.

Let God Be The Judge

When I was young my mother used to read to me. One of my favourites was a poem called "The Acorn and The Pumpkin". It told the story of a young man who walked outside one day to meditate. He came to field of ripe pumpkins. In the same field was a huge acorn tree. The young man meditated on the tiny acorns hanging down from the huge tree limbs. Then he meditated on the huge pumpkins fastened to the tiny vines.

"God blundered," the young man reflected. "He should have put the tiny acorns on the tiny vines and the huge pumpkins on the huge limbs."

Then the young man lay down under the tree and fell fast asleep. A few minutes late, he was awakened by a tiny acorn bouncing off his nose.

The man rubbed his bruised nose and thought: "Maybe God was right after all."

The story speaks for itself and needs little comment, except perhaps to say that, like all good stories, this is one which makes a plea. It pleads with us to allow God the better judgment and, in this way, to acknowledge our need of Him. For it is only when we do this that we can make progress in our lives.

I have found this to be very true in my own life, especially in my calling to the priesthood. It's a long story and I'll save the details for another day. For many of my years in the seminary I was of the independent kind. (There is a certain sense in which I still am.) But it was then an unhealthy kind of independence.

It was the independence that believes you can go it alone, without God. That kind of independence is really a form of imprisonment.

Outwardly I was a good student and a suitable candidate for the priesthood, but inwardly I knew that all was not well, for I was trying to get by on my own strength alone. It was only when, in a moment of grace, I acknowledged my own nothingness and my consequent need for God that I really began to make sufficient strides in the right direction, strides that ultimately enabled me to embrace the priesthood wholeheartedly at my ordination on 8 June, 1985.

So it was with Peter when he said to Jesus: "Leave me, Lord, I am a sinful man." It is only when we acknowledge our own nothingness that the adventure of discipleship can truly begin.

What happened to Peter can happen to all of us, and not just to those who are called to the priesthood or religious life. When we recognise our own sinfulness, the power of Christ becomes available to enrich us, so that we can offer ourselves to God, faults and all. There is a great paradox in all this, but it is true. *When we have experienced our own weakness, God can strengthen us.* When we have experienced our own emptiness, God can fill us. When we have experienced our own poverty, God can enrich us.

The discovery of our spiritual poverty opens our souls to receive what God is offering: it awakens us to an awareness of His call. We should not search for God in strange places but in the familiar surroundings of ourselves and in the humdrum bits and pieces of our every-day experiences. We will meet Him too in the midst of our pain, much more so than in the midst of our plenty.

When we thus discover the hand of God at work in our lives, the impossible becomes possible and the lowest ebb becomes the turning of the tide.

The Triumph of The Cross

Of all the Christian symbols that exist, the cross is surely the most popular. We live our lives surrounded by it—on rosary beads, on walls in schools and houses, often in the shape of older churches, around our necks, hanging from our ears, in the signing of ourselves at prayer, and so on. In fact, we are so surrounded by the cross that we could be in real danger of losing its meaning. There is the distinct possibility that for many the cross is no more than an ornament, a sort of "good luck charm".

There is also the possibility that we *only* associate the cross with pain and suffering. We speak, for example, of people having a "heavy cross" to carry in life. There is, of course, truth in this, but it's not the full truth. There is another very important aspect to the cross that we often neglect, namely, the element of triumph or victory that is also associated with the cross. The cross, as well as being a reminder of the pain and suffering which Christ endured for our sake and a reminder of the consequent suffering that we too must endure in life, is also a symbol of Christ's triumph and victory over death and evil.

The *triumph* of the cross is this great truth: after death comes the resurrection, after night comes the day, after winter comes the spring. It is the assurance that flowers can bloom even in the snow. It is the promise that, despite the apparent hopelessness of our situations, and the difficulty and sheer weight of our lives, we shall not be overcome! And that, even now, it is possible for good to come out of bad. In this way, the cross is always a blessing (in disguise), is always redemptive.

I came across a very moving example of how true this is some years ago. I was visiting an old woman whose only son had died in his teens of cancer. She spoke to me about the last days of his long illness and how, suspecting that he was going to die, he asked her: "Mammy, what is it like to die? Does it hurt?"

She prayed to God for an answer to his question and then said: "Son, you know how when you were a tiny boy, you used to play so hard all day that when night came, you would be too tired to undress—so you would tumble into my bed and fall asleep? That was not your bed. It was not where you belonged. And you would only stay there a little while. In the morning—to your surprise—your would wake up and find yourself in your own bed in your own room. You were there because someone had loved you and had taken care of you. Your father had come, with his great strong arms, and carried you away. Death is like that. We just wake up some morning in another room—our own room, where we belong. We shall be there, because God loves us even more than our human fathers and takes care of us just as tenderly."

We were both silent for a moment. Then she said softly: "My son never had any fear of dying after that. If, for some reason that I still don't understand, he could not be healed, then this taking away of all fear was the next greatest gift God could give us. And in the end my son went into the next life exactly as God had told me he would—gently, softly."

And there was a profound look of peace on her face as she spoke.

That's the triumph of the cross!

Somebody Said
That Somebody Said

I don't know who wrote these verses, who he or she was, but the words get straight to the ugly heart of gossip:

> *Somebody said that somebody said:*
> *Trouble was caused and suspicion fed.*
> *Someone passed on an idle word,*
> *Someone repeated gossip heard.*
>
> *Many a friendship has been wrecked*
> *Through hearsay poisoned and unchecked.*
> *Mischief was made and rumour spread:*
> *Somebody said that somebody said.*

I don't have many pet-hates, but I must confess that one of the few I do have is "hearsay". And what I find most repulsive about "hearsay" is the manner in which people attach so much face value to the things they hear, and how they pass them on with such authority and absolute conviction, as if it were unquestionably the truth, the whole truth, and nothing but the truth.

What I find equally hard to take is the tendency people have to hear only what they want to hear and thus to misrepresent the truth to others. It makes me angry, because it seems so unjust, such an invasion of privacy, such a violation of the truth, so self-righteous, so unchristian. I feel so strongly about this because it is a matter of urgency, a matter that calls into question in a serious way the quality of our Christianity.

But I do not propose to launch into a strongly-worded defence of the victims of "hearsay" or an equally strongly-worded attack on the perpetrators of this evil. Instead, I would like to suggest two positive responses which we could make to "hearsay" and those who carry it.

The first of these responses is based upon the wisdom of the Old

Testament. The author of Ecclesiasticus, showing remarkable insight, says: "The defects of a man appear in his talk . . . the test of a man is in his conversation . . . a man's words betray what he feels."

Jesus displays similar insight when he concludes that "a man's words flow out of what fills his heart".

Those who indulge in gossip and hearsay in regular fashion are often unwell and suffering people. Their obsession with cheap talk about the faults and failings of others is often an immature response to feelings of insecurity in themselves. Indeed, it has been proved by psychologists that the faults which we find most repugnant in others are precisely the ones that plague our own lives.

Taking Jesus at his word, we see that the heart which is filled with peace will speak words of peace, the heart which is filled with the love of God will speak words of love. But the heart which is filled with fear will speak words of fear.

Our response to those enslaved by hearsay must be one of Christian compassion. We should recognise their suffering and realise that they too are victims—victims of themselves and their own feelings of insecurity and low self-esteem. We should pray for them, that they will find acceptance—acceptance of themselves as they are, and acceptance of everyone else as *they* are; that they will realise we have nothing to fear from each other and that facing the truth (about ourselves) will set us free: free to live and let live.

The second positive response to "hearsay" which we could make is to treat it as such: mere hearsay and nothing more.

The story is told of the disciple who came excitedly to his Master. He couldn't wait to tell him the rumour he had heard in the marketplace.

"Wait a minute", said the Master, "what you plan to tell us, is it true?"

"I don't think it is."

"Is it useful?"

"No, it isn't useful."

"Is it funny?"

"No."

"Then why should we be hearing it?"

A Sin Is A Sin Is A Sin

There is a story told of a man who picked out six of his friends at random, and sent each a telegram that said simply: "All is known, leave town at once!"

Five of them left town immediately. That's a story which sets out to make this point: that there are few people, if any, in this world who do not have so-called "skeletons in the cupboard", things which have happened in their lives that cause them a certain amount of guilt-feelings and shame, past mistakes or sins.

It reminds me of a saying which we often hear: "If we were to have our sins written on our foreheads, none of us could afford to set foot outside the door."

Both that saying and the story about the six telegrams emphasise a very important truth: namely, that we are all sinners, to a greater or lesser extent. Sin comes naturally to us as human beings.

Sadly, though, people are fast losing their "sense of sin". Things which were once regarded as sinful are no longer regarded as such. Instead, we have become permissive, allowing ourselves all kinds of liberties.

> What used to be called modesty
> is now called a sex hang-up.
> What used to be called disgusting
> is now called adult.
> What used to be called Self-indulgence
> is now called self-fulfilment.
> What used to be called living in sin
> is now called a meaningful relationship.
> What used to be called perversion
> is now called alternate lifestyle.
> (from *Reality*)

We are making a big mistake. A sin is a sin is a sin. And sin is serious. It is damaging—to myself as a person, but more especially to my relationship with God.

Sin can take away our peace of mind, and leave us burdened by guilt, crushed by shame.

What can we do, sinful as we are? Where can we turn for relief? How do we find peace? The answer to all of these questions is Jesus Christ, the Lamb of God, the one who came to take away the sins of the world. Only in Christ will we find rest and lasting peace, because he has the power to forgive *all* our sins and to give us a new beginning.

And he loves to do this for us. He loves to forgive. He never ceases to long for us, even though we may have turned our backs on him and tried to reject him. He never loses faith in us, even though we may lose faith in ourselves.

So, as well as reminding ourselves of how sinful we are, let us also allow the thought of God's great love and mercy to fill us with hope. His mercy is a vast ocean in which our sins can be lost forever. No life is so ruined that he cannot build it up entire again; no heart is so withered and dead that he cannot refresh it and make it young again.

What You Long To Be

I came across a beautiful poem by an Irish priest-poet called Patrick O'Connor.

My Prayer

My prayer it is that I have friends
    In the streets where the poor of Dublin live.
For hearts have there the kindliness,
    The tender grace sad days can give;
And there is seen in faces wan,
    In weary eyes, a faith-lit glow,
As in a picture I have seen
    Of some calm saint of long ago.

In Dublin town, at the evening-time,
    In many, an old, high Georgian room,
They will say the hallowed Rosary,
    or in the church's ruby gloom;
And as through thin, worn hands the beads
    Move slowly, slowly round again,
Great were my joy if I but knew
    That my poor name was thought of then.

A shield to me and a comfort sweet,
    Whatever the road that must be trod,
Would be their warm remembrances,
    For these, indeed, are the friends of God;
And men, at the end, will see among
    Those to whom Christ a crown will give,
Faces that I have often seen
    In streets where the poor of Dublin live.

(Patrick O'Connor)

It's a poem about the deep faith of the ordinary people, the "friends of God". It's a poem in praise of their authenticity and genuineness, the kind of authenticity and genuineness that is born out of great suffering, "the tender grace sad days can give".

When I read it for the first time it immediately set me thinking of the streets where the poor of my own parish live.

I thought of that man who, between the nerves and the neighbours, has a hard time of it. Not that the neighbours are against him. It's just that he imagines they are, and he prays every day for peace of mind so that he can face out to Mass again.

I thought of the housewife who, because it was the end of the week and her husband had no work, could only afford to sit her family down to a dinner of chips and nothing more.

I thought of that woman who goes to visit her brother-in-law in prison, because Jesus said we should.

I thought of the widow who misses her husband so much, but insists that we are "fenced in by the love of God" and need have no fear.

I thought of all those people so faithful to the Mass and their prayers.

I thought of all the children.

I thought of all these authentic people, these "friends of God". And I'm thinking now that God has a word for all of them. It's a word of gratitude. He thanks you for your faithfulness and love. He thanks you for your lives of quiet desperation, for your suffering and your sacrifice. He thanks you for being so authentic.

For all of us who dream of becoming better and more authentic Christians, God has a word of encouragement. It's a word of encouragement that is accompanied by a steady look of love.

As a great spiritual writer once wrote: "It is not what you are, nor what you have been, that God beholds with the eyes of His mercy: but what you long to be."

It is the wish to pray better that is in itself a most powerful form of prayer. It is the dream of being a better Christian that is in itself a better form of Christianity. And it is the desire to please God that pleases God.

Loving Yourself

There's a certain exercise recommended for use with groups. Its objective is to establish trust, and an awareness of our ability or inability to trust others. The participants are given a list of activities and are asked to select the ones they would *least* like and *most* like to do in front of the rest of the group.

The list includes:

- imitating the crowing of a rooster
- giving a two-minute talk about your best qualities
- reciting a short nursery rhyme
- giving a two-minute talk on what you like most about your friends.

I've used this exercise on many occasions and invariably the one activity which most people *least* like to do is the "two-minute talk about your best qualities". Most opt for something safer like reciting a short nursery rhyme, something which doesn't cost too much. The last group of people with whom I used this little exercise discussed afterwards the reasons why they would shy away from the two-minute talk on themselves. They came up with three principle explanations:

(a) We had never thought of ourselves in terms of our best qualities–we would find it easier to think of our negative points.

(b) We hadn't the vocabulary to do it.

(c) We were afraid that others might think we were boasting.

All three reasons are most interesting and highly significant. They say a lot about all of us. They point to the reluctance which most people have to think or speak well of themselves. I feel sure that if I were to ask you to take some time out now to write down the three things you like *most* about yourself and the three things you like *least* about yourself, the chances are that you would find it much easier to list the latter three.

And yet Christ says: "You must love your neighbour *as yourself.*" We tend to overlook those last two very important words, failing to attach to them their full significance. We forget that being kind to ourselves, indeed learning to love ourselves, is a prerequisite for being kind to or learning to love our neighbour. We make the fundamental mistake of thinking that any form of self-esteem is dangerous and may cause us to commit the sin of pride.

It *is* dangerous to be too "full of ourselves", to have an over-inflated ego, but it is equally damaging to have no sense of our own worth as persons, no appreciation of how unique and precious we are in the eyes of God, the Lover of Life. False humility is as harmful and as sinful as false pride.

There are things about us of which we can be justifiably proud. We have been endowed with many good qualities and gifts which we have a duty to acknowledge and to be grateful to God for. Having a good opinion of ourselves is not being boastful or conceited. It is merely being kind to ourselves. It is being honest, and it is doing what Christ wants us to do. It enables us to trust ourselves and to be confident enough to reach out to others with equal kindness and trust.

If the Man Is Right, His World is Right

The poet, G.K. Chesterton, speaking about Christmas, once said: "God came down from heaven because all was not right with the world."

His sentiments echoed those of the prophet Isaiah, who spoke about the coming of the Messiah, and the two great gifts he would bring, two gifts the world desperately needed at the time of Our Lord's birth, namely, justice and peace.

It seems that little has changed with the passage of 2,000 years. There is not much evidence of that promised justice and peace, at least not on any world-wide scale. Instead when we look out across the world, we see disunity everywhere. Each day brings news of conflict, division, disharmony. Everywhere there is evidence of man's inhumanity to man. We live daily with the nightmares of places like Yugoslavia far away and Northern Ireland here at home.

Meanwhile, across the world there is the great problem of hunger, with thousands of people dying every day from starvation while more than £1 million is spent every minute on arms and ammunition.

This sinful state of affairs is further compounded by such added injustices as political oppression and corruption, crime in its many forms, poverty, loneliness and unemployment.

The world today seems in greater need of salvation than it was at the time of the first Christmas. In Jesus of Nazareth we see the possibility of being saved. He offers us a better way, a way out of the misery and desolation that we ourselves have largely created. Christmas is essentially a time full of hope. It is much more than nostalgia and sentimentality. It is serious business and it needs to be taken seriously, because it is our golden opportunity to live life to the full, a chance to make a change for the better.

It's just not good enough to despair at the situation we find ourselves in and to say that we can do little or nothing to change things on a world scale. Such a response amounts to nothing less than a "cop out". The only proper response to the enormous problems facing our world is one which begins with me examining the quality of my own life and faith, and making whatever changes are necessary. *If I don't change, my world won't.*

Perhaps a short story would help to illustrate the point:

The story concerns a Protestant minister in America. One Saturday morning he was trying to prepare his sermon under difficult conditions. His wife was out shopping.

It was a rainy day and his young son was restless and bored, with nothing to do.

Finally, in desperation, the minister picked up an old magazine and thumbed through it until he came to a large brightly coloured picture. It showed a map of the world. He tore the page from the magazine, ripped it into little bits and threw the scraps all over the living-room floor with the words: "Johnny, if you can put all this together, I'll give you a dollar."

The preacher thought this would take Johnny most of the morning. But within ten minutes there was a knock on his study door. It was his son with the completed puzzle. The minister was amazed to see Johnny finished so soon, with the pieces of paper neatly arranged and the map of the world back in order.

"Son, how did you get that done so fast?" the preacher asked.

"Oh," said Johnny, "It was easy. On the other side there was a picture of a man. I just put a piece of paper on the bottom, put the picture of the man together, put a piece of paper on the top, and then turned it over. I figured that if I got the man right, the world would be right."

The minister smiled, and handed his son a dollar.

"And you've given me my sermon for tomorrow too," he said.

"If a man is right, his world will be right."

A Funny Kind of Church

There was a time when to be a Catholic in Ireland was a very difficult and dangerous thing. I am referring to that sad part of Ireland's history known as the "Penal Days". In those days Catholics were forbidden education, were forbidden to own property, were forbidden to travel more than five miles without a permit, while the celebration of Mass was a crime punishable by death.

Things have changed a lot since then. Religious freedom is now a reality. The church has progressed to a position of recognised importance in this country of ours. But for all our "progress" I wonder are we any better than the church was during those terrible Penal Days? It is often remarked that the church thrives under persecution. This was certainly the case in Ireland, and it is still the experience of many countries where the church continues to be persecuted.

Of course, the danger is that once that period of persecution and punishment has passed the church becomes comfortable and complacent. The temptation is to live on the capital of the past, on the faith of our fathers. This could well be a problem for the church in Ireland: that we have become relaxed and even complacent about our faith.

The signs and symptoms of this complacency are many and varied:

- For many people, there is no longer any joy in being Christian.
- For many people, church-going is a chore rather than a privilege.
- Many people fail to see religion as a way of life as well as a system of worship.
- Many of us are lacking in enthusiasm for the Christian message.

If this is the kind of church which we are building, a church of stuttering and lukewarm Catholics, then it's in marked contrast to the kind of church which existed at the time of its foundation. That church was a living church: the people welcomed the message preached by the disciples, paralytics and cripples were cured, people accepted the Word of God and received the Holy Spirit—Christians rejoiced!

And not only is this present religious hesitancy of ours in contrast with the way things were in the early church. It is also in marked contrast to the manner in which we dedicate ourselves wholeheartedly to so many other "trivial pursuits", or display such enthusiasm for so many other things. The following lines express well what I mean:

> *Funny* how ten pounds looks so big when you take it to church and so small when you take it to the shops.
> *Funny* how long an hour seems when serving God and how short sixty minutes are when playing golf or bridge.
> *Funny* how hard it is to read a chapter in the Bible and how easy to read a 200 page novel.
> *Funny* that we can't think of anything to say when we pray and have no problem carrying on a conversation with a friend.
> *Funny how* we have so much difficulty learning about God and find it easy to learn so many other things.
> *Funny* how easily we find a reason for not going to church and never think of missing our night out.
> *Funny, isn't it?*

The True Story of Santa Claus

Along with a lot of other children, I believe in Santa Claus! I believe in Santa Claus because I believe in everything that he stands for—the magic and the mystery which surround him, the kindness and generosity which he embodies, the joy and happiness which he brings.

And I believe in Santa Claus too because I know that God created him! Here's the story of how it all happened . . .

How God Created Christmas A Second Time

Once upon a time an angel came to talk with God: "O Most Supreme Master, forgive me for saddening you. But I am saddened too. I have just come from earth where Winter is settling in and the celebration of your Son's birth is soon to take place. But nobody is talking about it. It looks like business as usual, and the day could pass unnoticed."

God replied: "Why are you telling me all this?"

The angel continued: "Well, I just thought it would be an ideal time, so close to your Son's birthday too, to work another miracle."

The angel hesitated because he knew that that was not God's favourite approach. God preferred subtlety. At last God spoke: "I must do something again to let my people know that someone believes in them. That I am not useless or old or beyond care. Help me find a new way to show my generosity."

The angel couldn't answer. He had been involved in so many real situations lately that he found little time to reflect or imagine.

So God continued to reflect: "I've given them so many gifts but that doesn't seem to make any difference to them."

The angel interrupted: "They're too busy. That's the problem. They're always going places, rushing from one place to another. Only the children seem to be free to . . . "

God interrupted this time: "Yes, that's it! The children. Something special for the children."

God was laughing. All semblance of sorrow was gone from Him and His red cheeks sparkled unusually bright.

Meanwhile, the angel was puzzled and observed: "The children celebrate all your lovely natural gifts. All is a wonder to them. What other gifts can you give them?"

It was God Who suddenly seemed realistic for a change: "Why, children love toys. I'll give them trains and dolls, teddy bears, building blocks, puzzles, games—toys for hours of adventure."

Suddenly the angel became excited: "So, you'll work one of your miracles after all?"

It gave God the greatest pleasure to say: "No! I don't have to. Children love mysteries. They love to wonder where things come from. So I'll encourage them to dream. I'll bring the toys late at night when they're sleeping. And I'll do it on the feast of my Son's birth, no, I'll do it the night before."

He could just see the surprise in children's eyes when they woke up in the morning. And He dreamed of all the toys He'd be able to make. God was just rolling in pleasure: "It'll be just like the beginning, at least for a day. Like Eden, like I always wanted it to be. And I know. We'll call it 'Christmas'." And so God worked eternally pleasurable hours making toys for His children to play with, to dream and wonder about. And come the night before the feast of His Son's birth, which all the world had forgotten, God put on His old red winter coat and hat and slipped into the memory of his people. Never to be forgotten again. For he comes every Christmas, a sparkle in his eyes and on his red cheeks, particularly pleased that He has gone undiscovered even to this day. A "Merry Christmas" from God, who created Christmas a second time.

I Abandon Myself Into God's Hands

Our world is a troubled world. We are all of us restless, searching for . . . what? We expect what we cannot even name; we are troubled and disappointed when whatever-it-is fails to arrive.

Our world is very like that which prevailed at the time of John the Baptist, in the days leading up to the coming of Christ. The Bible tells us that "a feeling of expectancy had grown among the people". Just as now, people were searching for something to cling to, somebody to believe in. People were restless, lost and alone, "like sheep without a shepherd".

God responded to this desperate situation by giving Himself. In the fullness of time, "the Word was made flesh, and lived among us". At a time when He was most needed, God made Himself available. He threw in His lot with all of humanity so that all of humanity might be saved from itself. In the words of a great saint, "God became like us, so that we could become like God."

That's what we celebrate each Christmas—the fact that at a critical time in the world's history, God made his entrance, as a little child. When we prepare to leave behind the celebration of Christmas for another year, we are reminded of the Good News that God is still with us, still madly in love with His people. He is aware of all our restlessness. He knows about our aimless wandering and He longs to lead us home, to that place of rest which is His heart. He would never abandon us, even though we might often abandon Him. He would never lose hope in us, even though we might lose hope in ourselves. He will always believe in us, even though we might find it hard to believe in ourselves and in our own feeble efforts. Why? Because He is God, and His mercy and loving-kindness are both certain and unconditional.

If, like me, you are inclined to despair at times; if you are given to thoughts of hopelessness occasionally; if you sometimes find yourself wondering where God is, if He exists at all, then . . . hold on!

It may well be that, in our panic, we distance ourselves from God, that in our restlessness and expectancy we have perhaps inadvertently allowed ourselves to move further away from Him.

Across the wide expanse of a bridge in America someone has written in large letters: "Does God today seem further away? Who moved?"

If we are honest, we will admit that we have done the moving, and that it's now time for us to move closer to home, by abandoning ourselves into God's hands and giving our lives over to Him completely. In this way we will find true peace of mind in the sure knowledge that God cares for each of us intimately.

There's a very beautiful prayer on this theme, called "The Prayer of Abandonment", written by Father Charles de Foucauld:

Prayer of Abandonment

Father,

I abandon myself into Your hands;
do with me what You will.
Whatever you may do I thank You;
I am ready for all, I accept all.

Let only Your will be done in me,
and in all Your creatures.
I wish no more than this, O Lord.

Into Your hands I commend my soul:
I offer it to You
with all the love of my heart,
for I love You, Lord,
and so need to give myself,
to surrender myself into Your hands,
without reserve,
and with boundless confidence,
for You are my Father.
                    (Father Charles de Foucauld)

Learning To Pray Better

There are many people in the world who are "great at praying" but not so great at being Christian. This is one of the biggest grievances which non-Christians and non-Church-going people have against us, a grievance once expressed by the great Indian liberator Gandhi. He said: "I like your Christ, but I'm not so sure about your Christians. They are so unlike your Christ."

What should we do to become people who can pray truly and in a Christ-like way? What is it that may be lacking in the quality of our prayer at present? I would suggest two things in particular for consideration:

Firstly, the person who wishes to pray effectively must do so with a deep-felt sense of his or her own weakness and sinfulness. This is the most basic attitude to have in prayer.

Secondly, this sense of my own weakness as a person should be accompanied by a corresponding sense of my own deep need for God.

I am convinced that if either of these characteristics is missing from my prayer, then it is certainly lacking in quality, and is in real danger of degenerating into a mere collection of "polite, meaningless words".

I am convinced too that the combination of these attitudes for prayer will certainly produce the desired effect of a more-than-adequate likeness to Jesus Christ.

This is precisely what Jesus noticed about the tax-collectors and prostitutes of his time: they shared a deep-felt sense of their own sinfulness and need for God. He remarked upon its absence in the chief priests and elders of the people, who were so full of themselves that they had no room left for God.

Jesus would like to see something of the tax-collector and prostitute in us. In particular, he would like to see that, when we come to him in prayer, we come with a deep longing and even a feeling of emptiness. After all, God cannot fill that which is already full.

The Devil Is Among Us

There was a time when it was traditional for priests and people throughout the length and breadth of this land to recite a certain prayer to St. Michael after Holy Communion.

The prayer went like this: "Blessed Michael the Archangel, defend us in the hour of conflict. Be our safeguard against the wickedness and snares of the devil. May God restrain him, we humbly pray, and do thou, O Prince of the Heavenly Host, cast Satan down to Hell and with him all the other wicked spirits who wander through the world for the ruin of souls."

That prayer, like a lot of other things, seems to have outlived its usefulness. In many quarters it is regarded as "old hat", belonging only to "pious die-hards". Indeed, it seems that for many people to "speak of the devil" in prayer form or any other form is no longer the fashionable thing to do. There are even those who would openly subscribe to the opinion that the devil does not exist.

Which is strange really, and sad too. Because the fact of the matter is that the devil most certainly does exist. The evidence to support this view is all-too-readily available. The signs and proofs of his work in our world are there to be seen:

- In the 50 million lives aborted worldwide each year.
- In the millions who die from starvation and the lack of basic health facilities while one million dollars is spent worldwide every minute on the weapons of war.
- In lives ruined or lost by drugs, alcohol and the perversion of sex.
- In people senselessly divided by sectarianism or family feuds.
- In people needlessly burdened by the guilt of their sins.
- In crime and violence, chronic unemployment, malicious gossip, greed and even loneliness.

In all of these, and in more besides, the evil one is at work. What a terrible mistake it is to think that the devil does not exist! The more we deny the devil, the more powerful he becomes.

44

What a cruel watering-down it all is of the life and work of Jesus Christ. Jesus never neglected to meet the devil head-on. Not for one moment did he deny his existence. For us to refuse to take seriously the existence and work of the devil is to be unfaithful to Christ. It is to be poor and pitiful replicas of the kind of person Christ was.

What must we do if we are not to be part of this "devil's denial"? We must, first of all, recognise how he works in our own lives. And we can be sure that he operates in the subtlest of ways, for such is his nature. For me, it may be that he instils doubts and fears about my effectiveness as a priest, or that he makes of me a priest who does not pray, so that I remain luke-warm and uncommitted.

Having recognised the devil at work within us and around us, we must stand up to him, strong in faith, as Jesus did. And we must know and believe that with God on our side, nothing can ever defeat us— not even the power of hell itself, and Satan, its Prince of Darkness.

The Mystery of God's Presence

Trinity Sunday is that day when we celebrate each year the greatest mystery of our faith: that God is Father, Son and Holy Spirit. It is not a day, however, for theorising or theologising about the nature of God. It is a day for gazing briefly into the mystery of God.

It is not a day for solving the mystery of how three persons, really distinct and equal in all things, could possess one divine nature, for many have tried to do this and they never succeeded. And this includes some of the saints.

The story is told that St. Augustine once set himself the task of solving the mystery of the Trinity. He decided to get up early in the morning when his mind was fresh and uncluttered, and take a walk by the sea to ponder this great question. Suddenly he came upon a small boy playing alone on the beach. He had dug a hole in the sand and kept running down to the sea, dipping his toy bucket into the water, and running back up the beach to empty the water into the hole. Augustine watched him for some time as he ran backwards and forwards, filling and emptying his bucket. Eventually he approached the boy and asked him what he was doing. Very seriously he told him that he was trying to empty the ocean into the hole he had dug in the sand.

"But child," said Augustine, "look at the vast expanse of the sea. How are you going to empty it all into that tiny hole?"

The child looked up at him and replied: "Much sooner than you will empty the vastness of God into your tiny little mind."

Augustine went home and gave up trying to unravel the mystery.

We can never hope to understand fully the mystery of God. All we can do is to catch a glimpse of God, wherever and whenever he is being revealed.

God is revealed to us in the Scriptures, especially in the pages of the Gospels. There Jesus speaks about God as a merciful and forgiving Father, and he speaks about himself as the Son of the

Father. He says that the Father sent him into the world, that he is in the Father and the Father is in him. The doctrine of the Holy Trinity is a reflection of this, for in it the church declares that Jesus is God as the Father is God. The church also says that besides the Father and the Son there is in God a third person, the Holy Spirit. The Holy Spirit is the mutual love between the Father and the Son, a love which is to be poured forth on all the peoples of the world.

God also gives us a glimpse of Himself in the lives of his holy ones. I'm thinking here not just of the great saints but of the lesser ones, the ordinary people who have been a part of the fabric of our own lives, and who have been for us mirrors of God's life and God's love. We refer to them as people "belonging to us", and it's a good description. It's only when they die and leave us here that we begin to realise what a revelation of God they were . . . and that as well as "belonging to us" they also belong to God!

One such person "belonging to me" died a few years ago. It's only now that I have acknowledged what a glimpse of God he was in our home. Over twenty years previously he had reached a critical cross-roads in his life: two roads diverged in a wood and he chose the one less travelled, and this made all the difference . . . It made all the difference because it was the road that led him to God and made him more and more like Him. It made all the difference too because it changed him completely. Through a life of deep prayer he became serene and full of peace. He came to treasure the love and companionship of others. He learned to accept his own human weakness and even to embrace it as his means to salvation. He became meek and humble of heart. He was the friend of children and the poor, and out of a generous heart he shared freely his time and possessions with all. He was a taste of the Holy Trinity in our home.

I tell his story here as an example of God's presence in our lives. All we can ever hope to do in this life is to catch a *glimpse* of God, wherever and whenever He is being revealed, to gaze briefly into the mystery of God by finding Him in the Scriptures and in the hidden people of this world.

Being Realistic About Christian Unity

A French historian was once asked why Napoleon was so great a leader. Was there any particular thing which won for him so many victories? The Frenchman replied that Napoleon was practical and precise. He always took action on a specific aim and achieved that before taking a single step further. Then he gave an example: Before going to war, King Louis XIV wrote to his commander – "You will please do all things which are deemed necessary so that my glory will be served."

But Napoleon wrote to a commander: "You will ensure that 15,000 reserve horses will be in Prague on September 14th. You will ensure that this order is carefully executed and controlled. And I will check it myself."

One message, the first, was very vague and achieved little, if anything. The second message was realistic, precise, and practical. And it meant certain victory.

Napoleon's precise, realistic and practical approach has much to offer if one is serious about achieving Christian unity.

Being realistic about Christian unity involves acknowledging that the miracle is not going to happen over-night. It means admitting that the day when Christians can worship as one and the same people, in one and the same place, and in one and the same way, is still a long way off. After all, our different traditions, Protestant and Catholic, are precisely that—they are very different traditions. And tradition is not something which we easily let go of. Being realistic about Christian unity might even involve acknowledging that it may never fully happen (to the extent that we can completely embrace one another in faith).

But that's no reason why we cannot continue to be practical about Christian unity, and to persist in taking precise steps in that direction. I'm thinking now of all the small but immensely significant things that are already happening in our midst, to foster unity among

Christians. Things like being able to greet each other on our streets, recognising one another not just as Protestant or Catholic but as neighbour and friend, sharing hospitality with each other, supporting each other's projects and plans, visiting each other's churches, being able to live and let live. These are the things that rarely, if ever, make the news. It's certainly a side of life in the north that people south of the border hardly ever see. And yet, it's happening all the time.

There may be even further practical and precise steps along the road to Christian unity which we could take and may not be taking. We could, for example, recognise, as St. Paul says, that "it is the same God who is working in all of us . . . the same Spirit that is given to all of us."

We could free our minds even further to realise that we have nothing to fear from each other as Christians, and to realise that what we have in common with each other far outweighs that which still keeps us apart. We could acknowledge that it is possible to live and work and pray together without necessarily forsaking all that has become dear to us, all that has become so much a part of us, in order to do so.

And then, who knows but we may in this way bring about Christian unity—the essence of Christian unity—in our time. We may not have to wait a lifetime after all, or give as much ground as we feared.

The Trouble With Christ

A Visitor

Christ came into my room the other day
and stood there,
and I was bored to death.
I had work to do.

I wouldn't have minded if he'd been crippled
or something . . . I do well with cripples!
But he just stood there . . . all face
and with that dammed guitar!

I didn't ask him to sit down,
He'd have stayed all day.
Let's be honest,
You can be crucified just so often . . .
Then you've had it.
I mean you're useless,
No good to God, let alone anybody else.

So I said to him after a while,
"Well, what's up . . . what is it you want?"
And he laughed . . . stupid!
Said he was just passing by
and thought he'd say hello.

Great.
I said "Hello."
So he left
and I was so dammed mad:
I couldn't even listen to the radio.
I went and got some coffee.

The trouble with Christ is
He always comes at the wrong time
and in the wrong garb!

(John L'Heureux, S.J.)

I'm sure that the sentiments expressed by John L'Heureux are ones with which all of us can identify. We have all known the frustration of people coming for help of some sort at an inopportune time. At such times we find ourselves caught in a tension between doing what we know to be the right thing and wanting to be left alone and not bothered. It's a case of "the devil or the deep blue sea", the classical dilemma.

Nevertheless, it needs to be stressed that the right and proper thing to do in situations where strangers chance to pass our way is to be welcoming and, as the Gospel teaches, hospitable. Of course, hospitality is a very different matter from what it was, say, 20 years ago. Those were the days when nobody locked their doors, at least during the day, and strangers were few and far between. Today the whole scene has changed. Today is the day of locks, bolts, chains, peepholes, alarm systems, dogs, and, in some cases, guns.

Yet today there is more need than ever for hospitality and friendliness. In the world today there are lots of strangers, aliens and displaced people. They move into neighbourhoods where they know nobody and where life can be very lonely for them.

Christ calls us to welcome the strangers in our midst. It's not just a question of keeping the doors of our homes open. It's more a case of keeping the doors of our hearts open, by welcoming them as they are.

The rewards for such simple gestures of hospitality are enormous. Christ himself said that even a trivial act of kindness, like giving a cup of cold water, would not go unrewarded. There are earthly rewards too, such as the growth of understanding, friendship, cooperation—things our neighbourhoods are crying out for.

For the followers of Christ, hospitality is not an optional extra. It is at the very heart of the Gospel. And the ultimate motivation is clear: to welcome the stranger is to welcome Christ himself.

Reconciliation

The story is told of the fellow who hadn't been to Confession for close on 40 years. One day he happened to be in Dublin and plucked up the courage to go.

He began in the customary fashion: "Bless me, Father, for I have sinned. It's near 40 years since my last Confession, Father."

Then, with some difficulty he recounted the deeds he had done. No stone was left unturned as he endeavoured to make a clean sweep. Even the most trivial misdemeanours got a mention.

After about 15 minutes of "telling all" he asked the priest for absolution. His request was met with total silence from the other side. Again he asked for forgiveness, and again there was nothing forthcoming. Finally, in desperation he begged his confessor to take away his sins.

Now his pleading eyes began to focus and he could see that the priest wasn't there at all. He could also see that there was a little old lady on the far side with her right ear firmly pressed against the grille.

"Where's the priest? the man inquired.

"I don't know for sure," came the reply, "but if he's after hearing half of what I just heard I'd say he's gone for the police!"

It's a funny story, but at the same time it says something serious about the popular perception of Confession today—or should I say the *unpopular* perception of Confession—which a lot of people seem to have. The sacrament of Reconciliation is not exactly the highest in the "popularity stakes". Undoubtedly for some it is a celebration of the love and the mercy of God, but for many more it is a "turn-off" and an unpleasant experience.

There are many reasons why this is so. I feel that one of the main reasons for the unpopularity of Confession in some quarters is the fact that unlike most other sacraments, this one is very much a "lone walk". For example, we gather together for the celebration of the Eucharist, Baptism, Confirmation, Marriage, and Holy Orders. Confession is, by nature and necessity, a much more private affair.

It's something where the initiative is very much left to ourselves. Maybe that's why it's not so well liked by so many people.

There is another root cause of people's reluctance in approaching the Sacrament of Reconciliation. It's a thing called *fear* and it manifests itself in many forms: we're afraid of the priest and what he might say, we're afraid of not being able to remember everything, we're afraid of being forced to talk about things we'd rather not talk about, we're afraid of God and what He could do to us. These are just some of the fears we labour under and they become the focus of our attention.

In the process, they distract us from the one truth we should be concentrating on, namely, that *God wants to forgive us*. I would go so far as to say that He desperately wants to forgive us. He wants us to feel forgiven, and to know the peace of mind that His healing forgiveness can bring. This is what matters more than anything else. This is what is far more important than any of our fears. This is what makes our fears groundless and needless.

This is what makes the Sacrament of Reconciliation such a precious pearl that is waiting to be discovered.

The Priest In The Modern World

The actor Alec Guinness was returning to his hotel in London many years ago. All that day he had been playing the part of Chesterton's famous detective priest, Father Brown, in a TV series. He was so exhausted after a tiring day's work that he hadn't bothered to change out of the priest's clothes. As he groped along in the dense fog, a little boy, obviously lost, wandered out of a side street and began to cry. Guinness stopped and when the little boy saw the priestly figure, he walked over, held out his hand and said confidently: "Father, will you leave me home?"

Guinness later traced his decision to become a Catholic to that incident, because he felt he wanted to belong to an organisation which could produce a body of men whom little children could trust so easily.

That was many years ago, and all was well with the priesthood at that time. Or at least that's how it appeared. Today it's no secret that the priesthood is in deep trouble and priests are undergoing profound change. Once the centre of parish life, priests today are sometimes thought to be standing in the way of progress. Once the most respected members of the community, today they aren't always trusted. Once they were the ones we were sure would be there, today we half-expect them to leave. Once the revered figure before whom we knelt for a blessing, the priest today is, in many cases, a confused person, wondering about his own vocation and his role in today's church.

These are just some of the indications that the priesthood is undergoing great change, but the story doesn't end there. There's another kind of pressure that priests are under too. It's the demand for diversity, the expectation that the priest should be "all things to all people". More and more is being asked of fewer and fewer priests. Of course, in this scenario the priest just can't win . . .

If his sermon is a few minutes longer than usual, "He'd wear you out."
If it's short, "He hasn't bothered."

If he raises his voice, "He'd deafen you."
If he speaks normally, "You can't hear one word he says."
If he's away, "He's always on the road."
If he stays at home, "He's a stick-in-the-mud."
If he's in the presbytery, "He never visits his people."
If he talks finances, "He's too fond of money."
If he doesn't, "No one know what he's up to."
If he organises functions, "He's stuck in too many things."
If he doesn't, "The parish is dead."
If he takes time in the confessional, "He's too inquisitive."
If he doesn't, "He never listens."
If he starts Mass in time, "His watch must be fast."
If he starts a minute late, "He's never in time."
If he is young, "He lacks experience."
If he is old, "He ought to retire."
And if he dies . . . "Sure of course, No one could ever take his place."

Under these twin pressures of the "changing times" and the "increased workload" the priest can choose to do one of two things. He can either let himself be overwhelmed by it all and give in to feelings of despair or else he can see it as a challenge: a challenge to renew his priesthood in the face of all the change he sees around him, and a challenge to get his priorities right in the face of all that is being asked of one man.

I share these few thoughts with you in the hope that it will enhance your understanding of priests and priesthood. I hope that it might help to remove the veil of secrecy and confusion that so often exists between priests and laity. I share them as a way of asking that you might always pray for your priests, especially for those in difficulty.

Pray for all of us, at this most crucial time in our history, that we may have God on our side and that we might be strong in the face of adversity and the powers of darkness. Perhaps these thoughts might just inspire others at a time when priests were, in a sense, never more needed, with so many sick to be consoled, so many sinners to be reconciled, so many injustices to be put right, so many false philosophies to be challenged, so many witnesses of God's love needed.

55

Mary, Our Mother in Hope

In 1950, just a few years after the end of World War II, Pope Pius XII proclaimed the dogma of the Assumption to the church and to the world. Europe and many other parts of the world lay devastated. Thousands of people had been killed. People looked in horror at the appalling brutality they had meted out to each other as nations. People wondered how cities could ever be built again, how human beings could ever live life meaningfully again.

It was against such a depressing backdrop that the Church proclaimed the dogma of Mary's Assumption, giving the world a vision to look to, giving people something to raise their eyes to, beyond the horror and despair of that present moment, giving an image of hope.

Are we any less in need of hope today? Do we not also need something to lift our eyes to, beyond the gloom of today?

Lengthening dole queues, the increasing number of our young people leaving the country to find work and life elsewhere, the apparently endless cycle of violence and counter-violence, the growing mountains of food lying around E.C. countries while millions die of hunger and lack the bare necessities of life, the ongoing problems of loneliness, sickness, and disease . . .

God has given the world a vision to look to. He has given us the vision of Mary who, in the face of huge questions to which there were few reasonable answers, stood firm. In her life Mary was not rendered immune to anxiety.

As Pope Pius XII reminded us in the dogma of the Assumption: "Mary during her earthly pilgrimage lived a life subject to anxiety, difficulties, poverty, and suffering."

There were times when she must have felt confused and fearful. But from the first visit of the angel Gabriel, to Calvary, and beyond, Mary remained faithful to the destiny to which God had called her. It was precisely because she stood firm that she was taken up to heaven.

In Mary we have the assurance that it is possible to rise above the doom and gloom all around us. In her we also have the assurance that there is more to life than meets the eye, and that there is after all a "happy land" to look forward to.

I had a friend one time who lived with this kind of hope in his heart. He died of cancer at the age of 19. I believe that, like Mary, he stood firm in the midst of great suffering and in the face of huge questions to which there were few, if any, reasonable answers. A week before he died he spoke about his imminent death as an event which didn't bother him too much, because he was sure that he was destined for a better place than this. The only pocket of resistance he experienced was the thought of leaving those he loved so much behind. Nonetheless, he lived out the last week of his earthly existence with that Marian hope in his heart.

The Feast of the Assumption, is a celebration of hope. It is a feast which addresses itself to all people in every situation, but especially those who find themselves at the foot of the cross, wondering what to do, where to go from here, asking what does life mean. Mary invites us to stand firm in our belief that we shall not be overcome, and that life is richer because of Jesus Christ.

Lord, increase our hope! Mary, be our Mother in hope!

Reflections On
The Giant's Causeway

The towering cliffs of northern Antrim overlook an extraordinary spectacle: some 40,000 dark columns head out into the sea, each formed with such geometrical precision that the place has been called "the eighth wonder of the world". For hundreds of years people have come here to stop and stare. Altogether, it is an astounding sight, set as it is against a four-mile stretch of cliffs that soar some 400 feet into the air. It is, of course the Giant's Causeway.

There are different stories as to how the Causeway was formed. One comes from Celtic mythology, suggesting that the Ulster hero Finn MacCool built it so that he could cross to Scotland on dry land. The geologists have a very different theory, but even theirs is tinged with uncertainty and remains somewhat incomplete. It is a place of uncertain origin, a world that is shrouded in mystery.

Since I first came to live and work in the north of Ireland, the Giant's Causeway has become one of my favourite places. What brings me there time and time again is the certainty of finding peace and tranquillity amidst the uncertainty of the rock formation. In this quiet resting place certainty and uncertainty meet, mingle and manage to co-exist. And you begin to see how the two are aspects of one and the same place, and how the other side of faith is doubt.

Which brings me now to the difficulty we have in equating these two. We find it hard to accept that doubt can ever be a form of faith. Instead we tend to think of ourselves as being somewhat lacking in faith because of experiencing doubt from time to time. We forget that faith is very much an affair of the heart. Quest and questioning are its heart-beat. Belief and unbelief are its two sides.

Without honest probing, faith becomes a dead thing, a jewel in a casket to be displayed on special occasions. It becomes a possession, an ornament. Faith is not a thing. Faith animates. It is a principle of life. Faith seeks meaning as a fish seeks water and a bird the air—to live and grow and be fulfilled.

Faith makes for dissatisfaction rather than for self-satisfaction. It is a stimulant, not a sedative. It makes the mind and heart alert and restless. It may lead to real agony and finally erupt into the only prayer possible: "Lord, I believe, help my unbelief."

To suffer from not being able to believe is the form of faith in our time—a discreet, humble, tragic, excruciating faith, but one that is sincere, honest and pure.

At the Giant's Causeway, there are contrasts and colours in the sea and in the rocks—as well as in the lives of all who go there. Those who visit this place will begin to realise that the contrasts and the colours, the mystery and the certainty, the belief and the unbelief are all part of the richness of life.

The Giant's Causeway has become both a source and a symbol of this insight for me. It has become a reflection of life's richness, a glance into the mind of God, a taste of time and timelessness, a hint of eternity and a moment of mystery—the mystery of faith.

First...again...again...and...

You could say innovation is our strong point at Bank of Ireland.

After all, we were the first bank in Northern Ireland to pay interest on current accounts when in credit and we developed a range of adVantage products with you in mind.

Other profitable opportunities followed, and there are more in the pipeline - which makes it exciting for customers and those tempted (and why wouldn't they be?) to switch from their present service to ours.
What will our next first be?

But of course, you are assured of more than expectations when you open an account with us - above all, the experience of how helpful, understanding and decisive Bank of Ireland can be.

All good reasons, surely, to call into your local branch for a chat with the manager, just as soon as you conveniently can.

Bank of Ireland

About The Author

Father Gerry Cleere was born and reared in Kilkenny, where he attended the Christian Brothers School, and was educated for the priesthood at St. Kieran's College.

He was ordained for the diocese of Ossory in June, 1985, and his first appointment was to the parish of Ferrybank, near Waterford. During this time he taught at Slieverue Vocational School and was also chaplain to Belmont Park, a psychiatric hospital which specialises in the treatment of alcoholism. He also co-presented a weekly magazine programme on Waterford Local Radio (WLR).

Father Gerry's next appointment was to St. John's parish in Kilkenny. There he continued his interest in religious broadcasting, presenting a weekly programme for close on four years, first with Kilkenny Community Radio and then with Radio Kilkenny. He also found himself back at his old *alma mater*, the CBS Secondary School, in the role of school chaplain.

At parish level, he took a particular interest in the field of adult religious education, initiating an Adult Religious Education Group which organised a number of highly successful parish programmes.

Father Gerry Cleere is a lover of all things Irish. He is particularly fond of the Irish language, having been a fluent speaker since the age of 15, and of Gaelic games, especially the fortunes of the black-and-amber! His other interests include music, theatre, reading, writing, and walking.

In 1991 Father Gerry was sent on temporary loan to the diocese of Down and Connor, his first assignment being in the parish of Holywood, Co. Down. He is currently working in St. John's Parish, Falls Road, Belfast.

He has maintained his interest in religious broadcasting and has worked with Ulster Television (UTV), BBC Radio Ulster, and Downtown Radio.

He is the author of *The Sympathy of God,* also published by Campus Publishing.